TURBOBLUES
or
Trinkets from my attic
Or...
It is what it is, accept it as it is.

by
John Grow

Turboblues.

ISBN: 978-0-6151-7838-7
Library of Congress Control Number: 2007909287

Revised Edition by the author April, 2009.
This is an original work of poetry.

introduction

A long time ago,
I began to set these poems to paper,
Convinced of their
Vital Importance.

I considered the words,
Noted the flow
From mind to eye
To mind to hand to paper,
And wondered
Who would read them?
When would eyes focus
On these words
For the first time?

So. Who are you?
Can you discern
Within this encryption
Committed to paper
The Real You?
The Real Me?

Wait till you find out the answer...

table of contents

the song of shakmir and arganach

AT FIRST, there were two realms, the spirit realm of light and energy and the dark and dense realm of matter. One infinitely light, one infinitely dark. In the spirit realm, energy moves in rapids and torrents of superfluidity, crashing and bouncing about, molding itself one way and another in no time. In the realm of matter, nothing moved. All was frozen as though of densest stone. So dense, time itself was lost in the past, unable to extricate itself.

NOW. Shakmir Herself bounces and bounds in the spirit realm. She moves with such power that She exits her realm and enters the realm of matter. Her godly energy hummed within and around the matter she was in. Slowly, the matter, unaccustomed to such power, ordered itself to the dictates of her light. And Shakmir took a form, as all things of the matter realm do.

SHE DWELT IN DARKNESS for an uncountable period. As she dwelt, the matter about her form loosened itself in the presence of her power and became fluid in her name. The time of the matter realm trickled from its lost place and swam in the ethereal soup with holy Shakmir, moving perpendicular to her matter form, but parallel to her spiritself.

AS SHE MOVED and the cold of the matter realm warmed and became fluid in her presence and time found itself, Shakmir was lonely in this realm of matter. Loneliness became unbearable and she willed her heavenly hands to work in the mattersoup, turning it around itself until it whirled and crashed almost as her realm would. She then thrust her holy hands into the soup and pulled it forth, molding it as she did into a form like the one ordered about her. And she gave this form her holiest song, singing to it until it reverberated in kind.

AND HER SONG WAS A PART OF HERSELF given unto her creation. She named the form Arganach and together they danced about and within one another, Her love reflecting back and forth to and from him she created.

HER SPIRITSELF GREW COLD, being so long apart from the realm of light which she knew. In haste, she bound from her matterself into the spirit realm to bask in its warmth. Arganach found her lifeless matter form and shook and wept at being without her as only a child would. In his sadness and desolation, he began to rampage about the matter realm Shakmir had made for them both. He shook until his matterself exploded, and he exploded with such ferocity that his pieces scattered about the matter realm like glass exploding itself into the sand it once was.

SHAKMIR REALIZED HER HASTE, knowing her creation knew nothing but the life she gave and would be lost without her. She bound back to the matter realm (knowing now the way to go), found her form and sought out sad Arganach. All she found were the bits of his form, scattered across the fluid matter realm. And as the pieces of a hologram are like smaller versions of the whole, so each shard of Arganach looked like him, only smaller. She wept upon the broken pieces, sad at the loss of her Arganach as only a mother knows.

SHE SHOOK AS HER ARGANACH DID until her matterself exploded, having the same result as poor Arganach. She bound back to the spirit realm (again knowing the way) and caused a trickle of the spirit realm to pour forth into the matter realm from the way she came. It poured until it found the way she made back into its own realm and flowed in this great circle, coming and going.

AND THE ENERGY FOUND THE BITS of Shakmir and Arganach and the bits formed themselves about the energy, with bits of Shakmir and bits of Arganach coalescing together into larger forms. And the bits of Shakmir sang to the bits of Arganach and the bits of Arganach sang back in memory of her song and his reverberation. And as time dictates to the matter when it must break down, the spirit energy finds its way back to its former realm to complete one circle, knowing it will circle back to sing the song of Shakmir and Arganach again as long as time flows free.

city zen

Noise! Noise! Delusion!
All this mad rushing about.
Clever illusion.

Man strives to order
But between the concrete seams
A tiny weed grows.

There's no paradise,
No endless pit of despair.
Just white noise. Nothing.

what is yours?

Cells duplicate
And die
And are carried off
And end up in your toilet
Or off your skin as dust
And this is happening now
And has since
Your mother pushed you out
And will until you die.

Given all that change over
And change out,
What exactly belongs to you?

sacred music

We are sound.
We are fundamentals
A half-step
Apart from one another,
Always a perfect fifth
From the one.

We are a chorus,
A chord in discord
Sympathetic raga of noise.
We are the word
Made flesh.

Living in constant
Doppler effect
Now to now
Shifting in phase
Between nowhere and nothere
Between matter and energy
As the shout
Reverberates
Along the walls of infinity.

scrutiny

Ignorance
Really is bliss.
Wisdom
Is true folly.

Eve ate
Of the apple,
Pandora opened
The box
And I
Cast a restless eye
To the horizon.

You got
What you asked for.
Fools.

Wisdom
Breeds scrutiny.
Scrutiny
Breeds curiosity.
Curiosity
Killed the cat.
Simple as that.

Notice
There are
No clear answers?
Nothing fits right
When you
Piece it together?

Don't think.
Don't piece.
Just BE.
And there is peace.

the avatar redux blues

If the great Avatar
(fill in your favorite)
Returned to the world,
So the set-up goes,
Who--Where--
What would He be?
Would He be a She?

It's the same
"You're wrong I know,
'Cause Jesus tells me so"
Hand-jive with a karma filter-tip,
But let us play anyway.

Nail holes and indignities
Notwithstanding,
Let's say Jesus
Returned to the fray--
Put on the meatsuit.
To be fair, his shake
Should be as fair as ours--
No better, no worse.
After all, that's what you get
For slumming it.

So the Son of God Reincarnate
Sits tonight in some bar,
Wondering where his disciples are.
Ears raw from loud music,
Eyes bleary from gin,
Musing at the wretched state
His life's been in.
He may never find
Till he peers through the mirror
At his eyes
That you're only as good
As your next life,
Not your last.

leaves

Hundreds of fingers
Splayed out from
Hundreds of hands.
Each one
Recieves the light,
Takes what it can get,
Gets only what it needs,
Stoking tiny green furnaces
Powered by the sun.

planck

A moment
Of Planck length
In Planck time.

Between is
And is not.

This is the nature of all things.
Of every thing.

Open--
Close.
On--
Off.
One--
Zero.
Is--
Is not.

God, you see,
Deals in pixels
This small.

god sings his song

God sings his song of love
To us
In the people,
The trees,
The beasts,
The plants,
The clouds,
Stars, planets
And particles.
In the firmament up high
And the deep below.

Infinite symphony
Of color and sound
And motion and light
Loud and soft.

Listen with your eyes!
See with your ears!

No music so sublime,
No painting so lively.
No poem so lyrical
As the great work
Writ infinite.

He is his work,
As are we all.

all that matters

Time Asserts itself
Beside, around and between
Space.
The stage is set.

Energy and matter
Interchange
And intertwine--
The metronome in motion.

Planets fall in eternal dark
About their crushing hot partners.
Molecules perform
their random dance
Grouping
And regrouping,
Losing themselves
In collective
After collective.

This is what it's all about:
Eternal dance
Across infinity.
All that matters.

all that matters (short)

Man lives,
Man loves,
Man strives
Man dies.

The rocks still loom,
Water is always water,
Mountains slowly smooth
And flatten.

That's all there is.
All that matters.

talking to god

One day, God asked,
"Why do you want money?"

I replied,
"So I can live and love you."

He replied,
"I give you life,
And I expect no payment.

I love you
More than you can love yourself,
And I expect no payment
But that you love me.

You can spend
All the money in the world,
And never find me.
I'm right here before you,
Free of charge."

I said,
"I don't see you."

He said,
"Open your eyes.
I am everywhere.

Everywhere."

praise

In a moment--
In a flash--
You changed my life
and my heart.

I once was lost
But your love has found me.
I am whole again,
New and uncorrupted
In your eyes...

invocation

What am I,
Oh Lord?

What is my calling?
What is thy bidding?

This is your call:
You are dust,
To dust you will
Return.
You are me and
I am you.
A riddle about
A broken mirror.

My bidding?
Act.
You think too much.

the world is good.

The wind whistles
Through distant trees.
The clouds part
And scatter
At ponderous pace.
The light
Of the sun
Dances across
My face.

The world is good
My love is with me.

The wind cools
My brow.
A kiss and
Sweet breath
from the one I adore.

The world is good
My love is with me.

home at last

Alone here,
I used to hate
Being in this place.
Anything anything
To avoid being here.

How can I explain--
Now I want to be
In no other place.
Nothing, nowhere
Matters more now.

end of time

Do not fear, my friend,
For at the end of time,
We shall all
Meet again
In a place
Where no shadows fall.

A place where we can
Soar
And
Skitter about
Like children
Across endlessly green
And winding hills.

Free to run,
Free from fear.

Free to laugh and sing,
Free from sadness.

Free to fly,
Free from death.

art

All art
Is self-indulgence
Disguised
As revelation.
Illuminating
Navel-gazing.

Expressive Pomposity.

Drum solos
Are very boring.

the way

Far too many books--
Too much information here.
Another dead end.

You will never find
The way to blessed Buddha
As long as you seek.

timmy

Yesterday,
When I last saw him,
He was so young.
Had to be yesterday--
A week ago at most.
Right?

He stood in the doorway,
Smiled,
And told me
"I'll be back soon."
He never made it back...

So many years go by.
So many new faces pass.
Age distorts everything--
Yet his face is clear.
Uncorrupted.
Time erodes
The finest features--
His are untouched.
Eternal youth
In the mind's eye
In trade for his life.

A vibrant boy
Boiled down
To name and numbers.
Yet frozen in a moment
Poised for greatness.
Facing the unknown.

time

There is something else
I must tell you
Old friend.

Time can be measured
In myriad ways--
In the pendular click
And turn
Of gear and rotor,
Or in the pulse
Of electrically charged crystal,
Or in the age
And decay of the flesh.
But these are not time.

Time is watching the gears turn,
The crystal pulse.
Time is pondering your old age.

Time is folly.

dark sunset

YELLOW WHITE
WHITE WHITE
BLUE WHITE
OF A THOUSAND
HEADLIGHTS
PASSED BY THIS SPOT
IN THE LAST HALF HOUR--

EVERYBODYINAGREATGODDAMHURRY GET THE HELL OUT OF MY WAY!
I'M GOING HOME!

While overhead,
And no one
Noticed this
But me
Parked by the roadside,
Muted hues
Blue, violet and purple
Dyed the clouds
Of indigo
While their edges
Were scorched
By pink-orange flame
From the retiring sun.

I try
To look
For these things
And take stock.

It brings me peace.

cumulonimbus

Coming round the corner
Past grand Bespin
Ensconced like the hall of the
Mountain king,
The space fleet was
Suspended
In eternal blue
Standing before the
Burnished grey anvil
Of mighty Thor
Awaiting his command.
All passed
At a stately, ponderous pace
As man scampers below
As his nervous rodent forbears did
To avoid sauropod footsteps.

9/29/04

Great branches
Of leaves
Bend and sway
In the cold wind
Like a silk sheet,
red, yellow, orange
In the light
Fluttering and flowing
across a new-made bed.

How can you say
It's not a beautiful day
Today?

turboblues

Sleek,
With sensuous curves
best seen in repose.
Her stance demure,
She betrays nothing
Of her passion,
Her power,
Her inner beauty.
Her voice,
Deep, smoky,
Is a whisper
And a scream
Simultaneously.
A roar to split the night
And pound the chest
In ecstasy unbounded.

rainbow hour

Painted lover
Awash in color
That shimmers
As she passes
The window
To meet me.

For a blink,
The magic
Within her
Revealed
With a simple
Sliver
Of glass.

i miss you

I wonder
What it's like
To see through your eyes.
I wish we were that close.

Though you're miles away
I feel your presence
Beside me.
Feel your hand shift
Imperceptibly
In mine,
And the soft back
Of your hand
As I imagine my thumb
Running against it.

I hear your voice.
"I love you so much."
I turn
To look in your eyes--
To drown there--
But you're not there.
I miss you.

i thought of you

The sky was hot--
Electric.
Lightning friction
Tore between
Air molecules,
Licking the sky
Like lovers
In a desperate
Explosive clench.

It lit the room,
A flicker in afterthought
Brilliant
As your eyes in passion,
Leaving me weak
In their embrace.

The clouds, demure,
Hid the tumult from view
While the rain fell,
Cool.
Not so much
A climax
As a plateau.
It would be a long night.

a woman's body

A woman's body
Makes most excellent music.
Fingertips, skin,
Teeth and tongue
Draw and glide
Rub and lick
Taste and hum
And she sings along
To the song I play...

michelle

You don't know how you look
When you're on your knees
Before me...

You don't know how it feels
Being inside you,
Stealing this moment
With danger moments away...

You don't know how it feels
Exploding
White-pink-hot
Within your clench.
Hearing you
Moan my name
In a hiss of passion.

I cannot love you, but I do.
I want all of you, but all I get
Is your beautiful body...

You tell me
Your heart iis mine.
But you lie--
Or you're just not
Honest with yourself.

How can you
Be mine mine MINE
If you still keep
His name, his ring,
His vow?

I have your body
On this day.

He has you forever.

kissing you

He cupped her face
In his hands,
Sipping the kiss
From her lips
Like cool water
To soothe a
Terrible thirst...

Of all the many names
Of God,
Hers was the one
Which spread
Simple bliss
Over his aching heart...

Having her
Was not
Possession--
Not capture--
But completion--
The restoration
Of that
Which was parted
From him...

a night

Staring up at the ceiling,
I see shapes mutating
Out of dark and light.

In this deep quiet,
I hear your breathing--
Feel it hot against my chest.

The sweat between us
Cools again.
We're slippery and warm
And moist and spent.

Your kiss is a mix
Of your taste and mine,
A little sweat, a little musk,
And places passion takes us.

You slide and twist.
In a jolt, I am alive again.

I hear your smile,
Feel your laugh.
A gasp--
We ride again...

fall into a kiss

How can you
Resist
Waiting velvet lips...
Expectant eyes...?

"Un beso, por favor?"

Faced with this,
You who champion romance,
I ask:
How can you
Not
Fall
Into that embrace...?

How can you
Resist
The passionate
Firestorm shockwave
Across the plain of your heart
!

Only a fool would.
Only the dead could.

memory of love

The shimmering colors
Of the fading sunset
Rendered her face in hues
Red, orange and purple.
All the colors
Of his love for her
Sculpted her face
From light and shadow.

unreasoning love

I love you.
I see you now in my mind's eye,
I cannot help the beating heart,
Can't stop the smile
Crossing me.
Gentle eyes on a face
Of unashamed beauty.

God, it hurts.
It hurts to look at you.

Because if I do,
And should our eyes meet,
I will be found out
For what I am.
Naked, undefended
Before your gaze,
My eyes a perfect window
To the perfect
Unreasoning love for you.

I mustn't look at you.
What if I do,
And I don't see
The same love there for me?

love was there

Someone approached me
Today.

Strange.
Looked like her,
Talked like her,
Smelled like her,
Smiled like her--
It WAS her,
But with
Something
Missing...

There was love
For me there once.

Did I
Imagine it all?
Did it
Happen at all?

Perhaps
It was all a dream:
Full of emotion
Yet devoid of substance.

It seems
This is
How it is
When love
Disappears
From her eyes
As though
It was never
There.

a trip one night

I had some weird shit once.
It turned everything I saw
Into a grainy
Late–night documentary
On cave life.

Formed around me
A painting
Of a desert after dark
With moon–dappled cacti
In a thousand shades of neon.
A great figure in black
Dragged me through this expanse
To the bright
City at night
Always at the horizon,
Never closer.

I saw the face
Of the woman I loved
Change a thousand times before me
Into the visages
Of the women
I wished for before.

I reached epiphany
At the end of my great sojourn
I wanted her more
Than my next heartbeat.

I told her so
But she didn't listen—
Or didn't hear.
She was in the attic
Of her own mind
Sifting randomly
Through her trinkets,
As I was in mine

my sweetness

I need
To touch your skin.

I need
To kiss your full lips.

I need
To feel your warmth against me.

I need
To hear your voice.

I need
To hold you and never let go.

I need
To live in a world where it's just
You and me.

Another minute has passed.
How can I bear
Another minute without you?

I need
You, my sweetness...

bad love

God help the man
Who falls in love
With a woman
Unfathomable.

God save his heart
As it trips,
Stumbles
And second-guesses
Down Love's path.

Watch from above
Over the love
Born of purest fury...

does god think…?

I fell
In love
Again
Today.

She doesn't
Know me--
Doesn't know
I exist--
But there are
Two types of people:
Those who exist in flesh
And those who exist
In the mind's theatre

Insubstantial
In the tactile sense,
Beyond that
Quite alive.

Does god,
Therefore,
Think
In impulses
Of flesh
And blood?

I think
That's why
We live
Even when
We die.

ultimatum

Do you know
How it is
To have
Your destiny
Personified
And--
Just--
Within--
Reach?

I can't look
Her way.
Every time I do,
Time stops
As my soul
Drinks her in--
For a loving glance
From her liquid eyes,
My life is forfeit.
For her touch--
A brush of her hand--
I give my self
And more.

I stare too long--
Get caught,
Blushing.
God grant me
From this world
Release
If you won't
Give me
The words
That would open
Her heart
To me...

the landing's a killer

Icarus soars
On cocaine wings--
Hit the stratosphere,
Watch the wings
Vaporize
In popping green fire.
Too high--
Never high enough.
The landing's a killer.

Foolish mortal
Aspires to godhood--
Ten seconds
On Olympus,
Then hurled earthward
By Zeus' hand.
The landing's a killer.

Try, try again
Baby boy,
Suck on the glass teat
For your succor,
Sucker.
Neck in the mousetrap again.
The landing's a killer.

green fire

Green fire
Burning with the sun
And summer heat
Around me,
Roaring skyward
In verdant fractal billows.
It is a cool flame,
Lush emerald
Stretching horizon to horizon,
Which hides from view
The sins of man.

love's opiate bliss

The hunger.
Sorrowful, empty hunger.
Nerves and skin
Ache in dissonant,
Weeping hunger.

Hunger for touch.
Hunger for warmth.
Hunger for long,
Lingering,
Slow and soft...

Taste.
And smell.
Love and skin and
Sweat and musk and
Perfume.
All of it dancing
In love's opiate bliss.
Your mind in magenta darkness with her.
A universe of two as one.

Food doesn't appease.
Drugs a temporary
Expensive abatement.
Doesn't even come close.
They work around.
They do not solve.

Forget it. Forget it all.
No distractions.
No tangents.
Nothing else substitutes
For what you really need.

Your mind in magenta darkness with her.
A universe of two as one.

ocean of stars

One night when I
Was very very high,
I went out to the desert,
Laid on the ground
And felt like falling
Into the sky.

The stars were like water,
An ocean of ghostly light
Using luminescence
To convey depth

And there I was
Suspended over this dim sea
Flying slowly over it
Lying naked
On the ground.

sex

I can't explain
The sensual wonder
Of making love.

Rich.
Full.
Deep.
Pink blossoms on red,
Swelling strings
Over deep hum,
Electric blue lightning
Into the abyss...

Who cares?

No one can take leave
Of themselves
Long enough
To face that power unashamed,
And stop thinking
About the fucking laundry.

Besides,
No one can be
That un-self-conscious,
That trusting,
Around another smelly, hung-up,
Neurotic, bitter, sweaty, fat--
And you're just as bad.

Stop thinking
About this and that
AND COME FUCK ME!

It's a moment.
Not forever.
The moment passes.
Revel in it while it's here.

nameless beloved

Did we
Once and always
Traverse the astral plane,
My thousand years
In a moment?

Did we swim the ether together
Once in some eternity,
My love?

Are you the spell invoked,
Or are you the word spoken
In a thousand accents of flesh,
My ever before forever after?

The one
Always behind my shoulder?
Ever around the corner
Forever out of reach?

Conjure your way to me
Once again and on again,
Nameless beloved.

Our love
Is a spider's web,
Is a gossamer thread,
That links our souls
Through space and time.

Our love,
Incorruptible,
Outlasts mountains.
Outlasts entropy.
Outlasts eternity.

spiderweb

This spiderweb
Is my handiwork
And does my bidding
More than a thousand
Bishops.

Would you worship
The spider's web?
You're looking
In the wrong direction.

a prism

A voice soft and dewy
Like the petal of a rose
In early morning bloom.
One look into your eyes
Leaves the heart
Aglow,
Palpitating.
You are a prism,
Collecting energy
And radiating love
In its many colors.
Without you,
The sun shines dimmer,
Colder.

Please don't let me fall
Far from your loving gaze...

to the one i love, not yet come

Every waking hour
You're in my mind,
Near me.

Though I can't see you,
Your presence is light
Shining me a path.

Though I can't hear you,
Your presence is a note,
A symphony of vibrations
Comforting me.

Though I can't feel you,
Your presence is felt,
Always warming me.

Though I can't smell you,
Your presence is warm bread
Just nearby.

It seems strange.
Do you feel these things too?

Someday we'll be together.
Until then I have these things,
Impressions of you.

when you smile

When you smile,
You don't just
Brighten the room,
Brighten my day.

When you smile,
Big, dazzling, joyful,
That childlike grin
Makes me smile too.
Even when I think
There's nothing
Worth smiling about.

That is why
I love you.

That is why
I'm glad you're here in my life.

That is why
I'm glad I lived this long.

Thank you
For that and more,
My sweet.

quixote

The day is cold--
Better to sharp the nerves.
My steed is tired
But worthy,
At the ready.

Lady love awaits
At the castle gate.
It's a prince she wants
But a noble man she will get.

I close my eyes
In the saddle--
My horse knows the way--
Alabaster skin,
Flaxen hair
And azure eyes
Greet me
Behind my eyelids.

The promise of her touch
Keeps me alive.
Her sweet voice--
Harmonic tone in my mind's ear--
Whispers dusky dreamy
In the wind.

Bending low,
I spur my mount to speed.
She is my destiny,
And she stands in wait
For no timid man.

what did i enter the world with?

eyes and ears and skin assaulted by light and sound and CHRIST IT'S COLD! and who and what and why and WHERE'S THE FOOD? and two plus two is four and a squared plus b squared equals c squared and your penmanship is not satisfactory young man and who brought beer and where is your license and registration? and will she go out with me and she wants commitment and she's having a WHAT? and car bills and electric bills and mortgage and cable and clothes and good lord he was just going to kindergarten yesterday, seems like and he's bringing her over to meet us and if I would have done this five years ago it'd be different now and what do you mean I'm a grandpa and when I was your age we had to WORK and boy it didn't use to hurt to get up and the time seems to move by faster doesn't it? and the blackness is closing in I can't believe he's dead I just talked to him last week and you know it's really not bad I can't see I can't hear hold my hand until I get over won't you?

the end

I feel
The end is near.
Cold, lonely
Black nameless fear
Like a vortex
I cannot pull away from.

How did I get here?
Can I get out?
Is it real?
Or can mere shadows
Paralyze me
So efficiently?

reflect for a moment

Reflect for a moment on your life.
Ten thousand moments splayed like
Playing cards before you.

What do you see?
Moments of wonder,
Hours of pain,
Times of righteous indignation
And sensual overload,
People and places you've known,
Like clips from a movie,
Complete with dialogue and blocking.

What's it all about?
A hundred branches
And crossroads,
The path studded with should'ves
And could'ves,
Why bother?

Cry no crocodile tears
For your life.
No one else is.

labyrinth

We are walking corpses,
Pieces of the living god,
Moving day by day
To the center
Of the labyrinth.

And like the labyrinth,
There is only one path.
Which we all walk alone
To the living god.

god is...

God is loving
As you must love.

God is forgiving,
As you must forgive.

God is mindful
As you must be mindful.

Love, forgiveness, mindfulness.
And let us not forget detachment.

God is detached,
Loving, minding and forgiving
All his children equally.
As you must be.

just remember

Nothing is separate.
All things are one.

Matter is energy is matter.
zero equals one equals zero.
Infinity is a closed loop.

Don't believe me?
Don't understand?

Consider
That the only
Real separation
Other than that
Which you create
In desperate delusion
Is perhaps
Weak electromagnetism.

All things are one.
Nothing is separate.

message of goodwill

Every morning there's
A message of goodwill
In the eastern sky.
It's never the same
Day to day.

Every night there's
A message of goodwill
In the western sky.
It's also different
Day to day.

Slow down.
Clear your head.
Read the message
Please.

cheyenne

I know
It feels like
I left way too soon.
But you know
And I know
God has a plan
And we're all in it
Together.

So tonight while you sleep,
I watch over you all.

It takes a lot--
A certain kind of good soul--
But this is my true calling.

So don't be sad,
Shed no more tears.
You have a life to live,
And I have a job to do.

I love you mom,
Always have, always will.
And we will be
Together soon.

Until that day,
I am the breeze
Past your ear.
I am the ray of light
When it's dark.

I am your guardian angel, mom.
I am always there,
Never far away.

mother

The first eyes
I saw
When I could not see.

The first touch,
The first voice,
The blood in my veins--
The basis of my
Existence.

I wake
And sleep
And live my
Everyday
In your sunshine.
In your love.

The woman cradled her newborn son in her arms. She was exhausted, but her heart sang and her tears fell with boundless joy as she beheld the black tuft of hair atop his wizened red head and the delicate fingers on tiny hands.

He was an angel. All newborn babes were, no matter how they looked after the ordeal of entering the world. Impossibly tiny and red and beautiful in this perfect moment so far from the trouble and strife. She wished it would last forever.

She looked up at her husband, who knelt beside her. He was a good man, and a hard worker. He smiled and held out his hands. "Let me take him. You need to rest."

"Yes," she said, handing the child to him. "I feel so..." and she was out.

Cradling the child, The man adjusted the blanket over his wife. He'd seen animals give birth, but had never seen a human child be born until tonight. The innkeeper's wife, who assisted in the birth, cared for mother and child and reassured him before she took her leave that both were going to be fine.

He walked to the doorway and stepped outside, regarding the stars above. He was a patient man where his wife was concerned.

She heard things, insisting that what she heard was told to her by angels of God. The child is special, they told her. He will be a great leader. The messiah. She was very matter-of-fact about it all. He took it all in stride. The men of his village told him tales of how child-bearing affects women, making them crazy. They laughed as they told of their wives and he listened, never daring to tell of his wife and the voices.

In any case, he thought, that ordeal is over. Once the census has counted him and his new family and they are back at home, everything can return to normal and he can go back to work.

"One day, my son, you and I will work side by side, shoulder to shoulder. All things will be good and we will be happy. You will see." He looked down at the child, and in the dim starlight, he could see the child looking up at him, regarding him with an almost thoughtful and weary gaze. It almost seemed as if the newborn was smiling patiently at him, as the rabbis did when they elaborated on their parables for the slower listeners. What will it take to make you understand, foolish man? There is so much to do and precious little time...

The child closed his eyes again and slept. Joseph shook his head and chuckled. Now it was he who heard voices instead of his wife! He looked at the child once more. Life is all sorrow and joy and misery and pleasure and pain and everything in between. That much he knew. What no one can know is the future. And only God can know what tomorrow will bring for this carpenter's new son.

epitaph

Do not weep over this body.
It is merely my last moments
Preserved in meat.
A broken tool no longer needed.

It's not me. You will not find me there.

You will find me
In the sunrise and the sunset.
In the flowering plants
And the blowing deserts.
In the icy wastes
And the heart of the cities.
In the stars above
And the oceans deep.
In a mournful tear
Turned to raucous laughter.
That's where you'll find me.

Burn this body.
Scatter the ashes with the winds
From the highest place.
Let it be absorbed
Back to God,
As I have been.
As I always was.
As we all will be.

Live now in love.
Live now in peace.
I am in the air you breathe,
In your heart's beat,
In the warmth of a hug,
In the touch of a hand.

Long after you have forgotten me,
I will be there with you.

the answer

Why do you look
Into another's eyes
For redemption?

What do you expect
To find there
That you cannot find here?

Why do you seek comfort
In another's arms?
Touch is a transaction--
Given at a price.
My embrace is yours
By default.

You hunger for
The seduction--
Seduce me.

Love me.

Let me
Love you.

Mine is boundless.
Selfless.
Satisfying.
Eternal.

applewise

Applewise,
Apple wise?
Like Edelweiss,
Rare, but in rarefied realm found?

Rarefied heights wise,
Wise isn't found
in dizzying alpine peaks.

Taste the fruit.
It's just an apple, Eve.
Snake, like you
Is the teacher of Adam
In your native tongue.

Like the apple,
It's all plain to see.
Just an apple.
Nothing special.

Anything else you feel,
It's not the snake's fault..

offering

I am the offering
At your altar
Eager to be consumed
In your flame,
Assumed to your realm,
Brought to the summit
In your innermost sanctum.

Sacred?
Profane?

Why run from one
And embrace the other?

We are the gift
Of the god we make.
This convergence of
Love, need and knowing
Is our mutual prayer
To ourselves
And each other.

Let us sing and shout
Into the darkness
Together.

trinkets
(a valediction)

Here is what I know.
An explanation
Bought with pain
And blood
And sorrow.

But like pretty rocks
And trinkets,
They only hold meaning
To whom they mean
The most.
Otherwise
They're just this stuff
You have around
For no fucking reason,
Far as anyone else cares.

Admit it.

Read this again,
Perhaps then
You'll understand
What these trinkets cost me
.

one more thing...

The eyes
That read these words,
The lips
That speak them,
The hands that write them,
Are not yours,
Not mine,
At all.

The you
That you think is yours
Is not.

What part?
What speck?
What molecule?
What quantum
Of that body
Do you think
Is your own?

Who
Is the you?
Is it me?

How do we really know
The difference?

www.ingramcontent.com/pod-product-compliance
Lightning Source LLC
LaVergne TN
LVHW050941080826
845145LV00004B/1363